The No-Rehearsal
Nativity

Barnabas for Children

Barnabas for Children® is a registered word mark and the logo is a registered device mark of The Bible Reading Fellowship.

Text © Janine Gillion 2015
Illustrations by Rebecca J Hall 2015
The author asserts the moral right to be identified as the author of this work

Published by The Bible Reading Fellowship
15 The Chambers, Vineyard
Abingdon OX14 3FE
United Kingdom
Tel: +44 (0)1865 319700
Email: enquiries@brf.org.uk
Website: www.brf.org.uk
BRF is a Registered Charity

ISBN 978 0 85746 366 1
First published 2015
10 9 8 7 6 5 4 3 2 1 0
All rights reserved

Acknowledgements
Unless otherwise stated, scripture quotations are taken from the Contemporary English Version of the Bible published by HarperCollins Publishers, copyright © 1991, 1992, 1995 American Bible Society.

Every effort has been made to trace and contact copyright owners for material used in this resource. We apologise for any inadvertent omissions or errors, and would ask those concerned to contact us so that full acknowledgement can be made in the future.

A catalogue record for this book is available from the British Library

Printed by Gutenberg Press, Tarxien, Malta

The No-Rehearsal Nativity

a church nativity resource with a difference

Janine Gillion

Dedicated to all the children who have ever been part of a No-Rehearsal Nativity and the children yet to be so, and to all the young-at-heart adults who have joined in and enabled children to experience the joy and wonder of the true Christmas

Important information

Photocopying permission

The right to photocopy material in *The No-Rehearsal Nativity* is granted for the pages that contain the photocopying clause: 'Reproduced with permission from *The No-Rehearsal Nativity* by Janine Gillion (Barnabas for Children, 2015) www.barnabasinchurches.org.uk', so long as reproduction is for use in a teaching situation by the original purchaser. The right to photocopy material is not granted for anyone other than the original purchaser without written permission from BRF.

The Copyright Licensing Agency (CLA)

If you are resident in the UK and you have a photocopying licence with the Copyright Licensing Agency (CLA) please check the terms of your licence. If your photocopying request falls within the terms of your licence, you may proceed without seeking further permission. If your request exceeds the terms of your CLA licence, please contact the CLA directly with your request. Copyright Licensing Agency, Saffron House, 6–10 Kirby Street, London EC1N 8TS UK, Tel: 020 7400 3100, email cla@cla.co.uk; web www.cla.co.uk. The CLA will provide photocopying authorisation and royalty fee information on behalf of BRF.

BRF is a Registered Charity (No. 233280)

Contents

Setting the scene 6

Christmas at the heart of the community 7

Is this book for me? 9

A note about directed drama 10

Nothing can go wrong 11

Let's get this show on the road! 15
    The team 15
    Team members at a glance 17
    The admin 18
    The costumes 18
    Real baby or doll? 19

Including the Christingle 20

Including the blessing of the crib 25

Encouraging everyone to join in 27

The No-Rehearsal Nativity script 29

The (Almost) No-Sew Nativity 41

Appendices

Sample service sheet 52

Costume diagrams 57

Setting the scene

I would love to introduce myself before we begin. My name is Janine and I am a vicar's wife. However, I first met my husband at drama school. On leaving college, he was an actor for twelve years before being called to the Anglican Church.

We have always encouraged the full participation of children in the church and, even though our own children are grown, we still work to see children being both catered for and valued as a vital part of the life of church communities.

Throughout my working life I have enjoyed combining my professional work as an actor and teacher with my life as the wife of the vicar. I love Christmas-time and have always got involved in the church's festivities—including, of course, the nativity play.

When it was suggested that I write a manual to help others engage children in a nativity play, I thought it might seem presumptuous of me, as many churches, schools and other Christian groups produce the most wonderful, inspiring and enchanting nativities. However, I wanted to use my experience of all aspects of the preparation and performance, in order to provide a full guide for those who are starting from scratch, offer suggestions to those who want to adapt or develop their usual way of presenting a nativity, and be of use to those who may be interested in trying a different approach.

I have introduced the 'No-Rehearsal Nativity' into many different parishes and ministries, including a tiny rural parish in Norfolk, a large team parish in Richmond, a multicultural and bilingual parish in Hong Kong, a high-security prison in Hong Kong, numerous school assemblies, an adult blind and deaf church, and large and small churches in both inner-city and suburban London parishes. Each performance has been unique, and it has always been one of the highlights of the church's Christmas celebrations.

It is because each church is unique that I was encouraged to write about every aspect of the No-Rehearsal Nativity so that it can be tailored to your particular needs. You will see that I have also incorporated a blessing of the crib and Christingle service. Presented along with a nativity play, this is a format that offers a wonderfully rounded experience to all who attend, but, of course, it can also stand alone.

I hope that this book is helpful to you. I have had wonderful times sharing the nativity with children, and I wish you every blessing as you celebrate the incredible gift that God gave us in Jesus, and as you seek to share his love through the story of Christ's birth.

Janine Gillion

Christmas at the heart of the community

For many churches, the No-Rehearsal Nativity could be the very vehicle needed to bring the church into the forefront of the community, welcoming the community in a gentle and joyful way into the heart of the Christian church.

For some churches, Christmas is a time when their children are 'lost' because they are away visiting relatives or at home entertaining relatives who are visiting them. However, by the same token, it can also be a time when visiting children arrive at a church service.

It has been a joy in my parish work to watch how the number of children coming to the No-Rehearsal Nativity grows with every Christmas that passes. It's equally wonderful to see both home church and visiting children join together to create something beautiful to lift everyone's heart. Regular young visitors happily bound in, announcing that they are back! How wonderful it is when a child feels that their 'Christmas church' is just as much their own as their home church.

When your church community is able to put Jesus at the heart of the secular community, it also creates an opportunity to welcome those who may be nervous of returning to church, or those who have never before been introduced to church.

Getting organised

Christmas is a wonderful opportunity for adults to get together to create something that children and the whole community can enjoy. It is an understatement to say that Christmas is a special time for the church and for children, but it is sometimes challenging for adults to give children an experience of the real reason for the season, with the pervasive encroachment of commercialism ever ready to overwhelm us.

No matter how often we say that, this year, we are going to be on top of our planning, December always seems to be a month when there are just not enough hours in the day. Organising a nativity service during this busy time can seem like a daunting experience, but it really need not be.

Read through this book and know that, with the spirit of excitement flowing from the organisers and storyteller, everyone can not only celebrate the birth of Christ in an exciting way but also give priceless memories to the children who come along.

Is this book for me?

If you answer 'Yes' to any of the questions below, then this book is definitely for you.

- Do you want to hold a nativity service but are not sure how?
- Do you feel you have little confidence in staging a performance?
- Do you think that you haven't got the time to organise everything?
- Do you think that you have no time for rehearsals?
- Do you think it will be too difficult for your children to rehearse and learn lines?
- Do you want to welcome visiting children but need a way of doing so?
- Do you think you have no resources or that it is simply too big a task?
- Do you think you won't have enough children there?
- Do you think you will have too many children there?
- Do you want to try something different at your Christmas services this year?
- Do you want the children in your church to experience the true meaning of Christmas?
- Do you want to enable families to have a special time at Christmas that is meaningful and enjoyable for all?

If you have never attempted a nativity, or if you do one each year but they are not working and no one looks forward to them, I hope to encourage you.

Small churches might feel that it is too much of a struggle to host a nativity play because they lack the resources. On the other hand, big churches may feel that it would be impossible to accommodate all of their children. Please don't let either of these scenarios put you off.

It goes without saying that those who lead the No-Rehearsal Nativity need a generous and loving spirit in order to make the night special. My husband has a saying that always helps me: 'God doesn't call the equipped. He equips the called.'

A note about directed drama

For those who haven't come across directed drama before, may I take a minute to explain? Directed drama is just what it says—a drama that is directed as part of the performance. There are no rehearsals. The director or storyteller tells the story while the children react to what he or she is saying.

If the story requires the actors to move somewhere during the performance, the director tells them where to go as part of the story—for example, 'Then Joseph got up and went to sit with Mary.' The only thing the children need to do is listen very carefully to the storyteller/director so that they hear when it is the turn of their character to react to what is being said.

The storyteller can also speak for the actors, so the actors can be in a play without the pressure of learning lines or worrying about missing rehearsals. If the storyteller is speaking for them (for example, 'Gabriel went to Mary and asked her if she would be the mother of God's Son; Mary replied that she would'), they can simply react to what is said.

One of the main benefits of directed drama is that the children are less likely to be nervous and, therefore, more willing to take part. Even children who don't normally put themselves forward can happily take part, as they don't feel that an Oscar-winning performance is expected.

If you have children involved in the nativity who are comfortable and confident with drama and are able to ad-lib or learn a few lines, this is a huge blessing. However, it is important to make sure that one or two children don't dominate completely and take over the evening.

In the No-Rehearsal Nativity, the storyteller is in control. One of our Sunday school children sang a solo at her school concert one year—a beautiful lullaby to Jesus. Our storyteller decided to work the song into the script, which brought something a little different to the story and was loved by everyone.

There is always a chance, of course, that you have a child who wants to play all the parts and interrupts the storyteller all the time. In this case, the storyteller will probably know the child and can channel him or her into balanced participation.

Nothing can go wrong…

A nativity play is a gift to the children and their families, a blessing to all others who come to watch, and also a gift to God, so it should be full of joy. It is important for those who are preparing and organising the nativity to enjoy the experience as much as the children do. Joy is the main ingredient of the No-Rehearsal Nativity and prayerful calm is the way to achieve it.

Setting the atmosphere for the evening is the most important thing.

When I stand looking at the expectant children and adults in the cast, and all the mums, dads, grannies, grandads and carers who have come to support them, I can almost read thought bubbles above their heads.

'Why does Sophie insist on being a king?'

'What if Tom decides he won't stay with me and wants to crawl to his sister?'

'Please, God, don't let Joe fiddle with his nose!'

'Lord, can you persuade Brian to be a shepherd this year and not a cat like last year?'

'I hope Ben does what he's told instead of running round the church being an aeroplane.'

'Why is my child looking grumpy when she's supposed to be sweet and smiling?'

These are just some of the things that parents and I have laughed about, once they've realised that they had no need to worry. On saying 'goodbye' after the service, the adults are always keen to say how thankful they were for the words I use in the welcome: 'Nothing can go wrong.' I truly believe this, and I have always been proved right.

When I say 'Nothing can go wrong', I am really putting to bed other people's perceptions of what the word 'wrong' means. I agree that children leaping up and running across the high altar would be 'wrong', but it would be very, very rare for something like this to happen. My reason for saying it clearly at the start is that this gives everyone permission to relax and gives them confidence in the storyteller who is leading the service. When things happen that are unplanned or even challenging (for children are unpredictable), if the storyteller handles the situation without making it into a problem, then no one need be any the wiser and the disturbance is minimised.

If everyone has been told that nothing can go wrong, stress levels decline and both the children and their families can relax, leaving the team to deal with anything that happens during the event. This is not an 'anything goes' attitude, and it doesn't mean that difficult behaviour or behaviour not in the spirit of the occasion will be tolerated. It simply means that we try not to see every incident as a problem; we can adapt or pause, if and when it is necessary.

Whether you are about to present your first nativity play or whether you want to adapt the way you perform your annual play, we all know that children will be children. Some may be shy, which can be sweet, and with gentle persuasion they can be charmed into joining in. However, shyness sometimes presents itself as belligerence. If this happens, it is important to reassure the parents or carers with kind words and allow the child space. In my experience, children who behave like this one year will inch forward year by year until they are fully involved. It is therefore really important that, whether these children are taking part or watching, we value each one.

Then there are the runners, and the 'I don't want to be here' ones, and the 'This is for babies' ones! Whenever I meet a child who is a little challenging, I always remember that it is the church's and, more importantly, God's welcome that we are giving. The children and their families need to take away positive memories, as a negative experience at a young age can scar their thoughts about church and God for a long time.

If little ones absolutely refuse to put on a costume, even though Mum might be desperate for them to take part, assure them that they can still join in at any point, whether they are in costume or not. An anxious parent often makes the child anxious in turn, so reassure the parent and try leaving a costume with them. It may be that the child does not feel settled around unfamiliar people, or that they have just been refused something they want, or that the excitement of Christmas has overcome them.

If we say that 'nothing can go wrong', we have to believe it and act as if it really is true. If we, as nativity team leaders, start out with this attitude, it will help us to have an abundance of gentle grace and a good sense of humour, so that the little things don't overwhelm us or distract us from the message and the joy of the service.

Let me give some examples from my own experience.

- At the beginning of one service, I met a child I had never seen before who had come dressed as a donkey. I was thrilled, as we had never had a donkey in the play before. When, with great joy, I called for the faithful donkey to come and walk with Mary and Joseph to Bethlehem, there was no response. I walked among the children and congregation, saying into the microphone, 'Where is my wonderful donkey? I'm sure he was here a minute ago!' I saw a hand go up at the back of the church, only to find that the donkey had decided he wanted to be a king and had gone off and changed! Instead of this being a problem or embarrassing or disturbing for the child, it was actually funny and a bit of a joke on the storyteller. It was sweet that the new king had been shy to own up to his new character, and all was well because I was able to say that we were looking forward to seeing the handsome king later. The audience were able to smile, and the donkey/king knew that he was not in trouble for changing his costume.
- One year, a beautiful toddler angel spent the whole time 'flying' around the church, flapping his wings. Thankfully he wasn't noisy; in fact, he was charming and, by not drawing attention to him but letting him just get on with it, the rest of us were also able to get on with what we were doing. Had he been a noisy angel, we would have had to think again.

- Only last year, another toddler wanted to be a cat and, with her big fluffy cat's hat on, she also wandered around. She wandered in among the shepherds, walked up behind the kings and sat at Mary's feet when baby Jesus was born. She was enchanting and, for the most part, we just quietly enjoyed her being there as she got on with her own agenda. However, there was a moment when she went over to the fire bucket—with hands behind her back, she bent over and her head almost disappeared in the bucket. It was one of those moments when we just paused briefly to notice her, enjoy the picture and resume without allowing it to become a big distraction. That year, we were asking the congregation to join in a call-out (see page 27). I simply looked at the cat, then at the audience, and, in a stage whisper, said, '*Truly amazing*', to which they whispered back, '*Amazing*'. We then moved forward with no further comment.

What do you do about crying babies?

I wish I had a foolproof answer, but I know that diplomacy is needed, and a key part of it is in the way the parent or carer and baby are approached. Parents with babies often feel pressured and may well be having to split their attention between the baby and another child or children who are participating. They also have lots of stuff to deal with—pushchairs, bottles, toys, bags, and so on. Some may be acutely aware that their baby is disturbing others and may be fearful of making a fuss and being noticed.

Other mums, I believe, don't realise how disturbing their baby's cry can be. They are in the middle of the situation, dealing with the baby and unable to focus on the bigger picture. A mother might even present herself as a challenge to the church, saying, in effect, 'My baby is just as important as anyone else, so you will have to put up with it.'

What each church needs is a children's champion. This special person is someone who can seek out the mum with a big smile and, before anything else, engage mother and baby in compliments and congratulations so that the mother is not on the defensive. She will then feel that she and her baby are important and will allow your children's champion to work with them to help. If the mum feels comfortable and supported, there will be a way into the situation. If she is stressed, it is likely that her baby will catch the emotion and the situation may escalate.

Ask how you can help. If the baby is crying in the pram and she has other children to watch in the play, ask if you can walk the baby around the church. If you don't know the mum, stay in her sightlines, in order to reassure her and protect yourself. She may let you hold the baby. In my experience, a new smiling face to look at often shocks a baby into silence. One trick that a friend of mine used, which worked like a dream, was to bring out a plastic mirror and, if the baby was old enough to focus on it, show them their own face.

Alternatively, you could ask the mother to go with you to the back of the church, assuring her that she will still be able to see the play and that you can offer an extra pair of hands to carry her things. Keep pointing out that you don't mind, but the children taking part in the play might find it hard to hear the storyteller.

If a mother is anxious because the baby needs feeding and she is not comfortable about feeding in situ, help her to find a more private place.

The rule is always to affirm. However, if a situation becomes seriously disruptive and just too difficult to handle, you may need to be kind but firm in asking a mum to consider the other children and go somewhere where the baby cannot be heard, such as the vestry. It's about allowing the story to flow and making sure that the children who are involved feel comfortable and safe to enjoy themselves.

Let's get this show on the road!

The team

How much help will be needed? This will depend, of course, on your own church or organisation, but the old motto 'Many hands make light work' is true. However, your helpers must be people who want to be there; a begrudging spirit will not lead to a great event.

A complete 'at-a-glance' list of people needed to help can be found on page 17.

It is wonderful when the priest, vicar or head teacher (if the performance is taking place in a school) wants to take part as a performer, but it is not a problem if they don't. It is desirable for them to be there to welcome people, though, as their presence endorses and gives confidence to those who are preparing and performing.

> Note
>
> If you do have a participating church leader, the role of the angel Gabriel (the bringer of good news) is worth considering for them. Gabriel explains to Mary that she is to have God's baby and reassures her that Joseph will still want to marry her. He is there from the beginning to the end of the play, walking with Mary and Joseph as their constant guide, and can play a part in directing other characters to their places. This all means that the role of Gabriel would suit a confident adult who is unafraid to ad-lib.

The storyteller

It goes without saying that the pivotal role in the No-Rehearsal Nativity is that of the storyteller. The person who takes this role, be they clergy or laity, is the main focus and needs to be someone to whom the children can relate.

When deciding who is to be the storyteller, there are a few pointers to be kept in mind. The storyteller needs to be someone who:

- definitely wants to take the role
- exudes kindness
- has an open, welcoming and encouraging smile
- doesn't panic easily and always looks unflustered (however they are feeling)
- is able to speak with confidence to both adults and children
- can use a script but will not be bound by it
- is passionate about helping the children and adults to have a truly spiritual and enjoyable experience

Supporting adults

Although the No-Rehearsal Nativity is primarily for children, it is well worth having a few adults who are prepared to dress up and act to support the children.

A word to the wise here is that the adults who take part should not only be confident but should also know that they are there to enhance the children and help them shine rather than taking the limelight themselves. This is quite a skill, but we all know people who are natural encouragers of children, so invite them to do what they do best and join in. They might be parents but don't need to be. However, they do need to dress up.

I would suggest that you have one adult in each of the groups of actors—angels, shepherds, and so on—who will travel around the church with the children. The children will then know that they don't have to remember when, where or how to move; they are being led and can enjoy the moment.

Welcomers

When thinking about the No-Rehearsal Nativity or, indeed, any service, we all know that the welcome is important to set the scene so that everyone is comfortable and excited.

Place people at the door to welcome and greet everyone with a smile. Your welcomers will need to be briefed about a few important things they must do:

- Make sure that people involved in the play can be directed or taken to a place where they can get ready.
- Make sure that new children are welcomed as warmly as those you know.
- Make sure the adults have service sheets or are told what will be happening.

Team members at a glance

Preparation team

◊ Church leader
◊ Church administrator
◊ Chief organiser
◊ Costume gatherers and makers
◊ Ironers
◊ Set-up crew

If you are including Christingles, you'll also need the following:

◊ Someone to buy oranges, red electrical tape, cocktail sticks, raisins/sweets, candles and kitchen foil
◊ A team of children and adults to make the Christingles the day before

On the night

◊ Church leader
◊ Storyteller
◊ Welcomers
◊ Organist/pianist
◊ Singers (optional, but they really make a difference)
◊ Chief organiser and set-up crew
◊ Costume dressers and collectors
◊ Adult actors
◊ Safety champion (assigned to check the fire extinguishers and set bowls of damp towels in strategic places)
◊ Children's champion
◊ People to say farewell and clear away

The admin

Advertising

You will need posters to advertise your play on church noticeboards, to give to the local schools and to display in community outreach areas. The details need to be specific, and make sure you add a sentence to let everyone know that you already have a Joseph and Mary (see below).

Service sheets

I have always included carols in the No-Rehearsal Nativity, not only because many people look forward to singing the seasonal favourites but because they can be specifically chosen to illustrate the story and lend atmosphere. In practical terms, they also give the children time to move around the church and get into position in preparation for their entrances.

A specially printed service sheet works best, including all the words of the songs and prayers, as juggling hymn books and children can be difficult. The suggested format on pages 52–53 can be used or adapted. (This service sheet is designed to be photocopied back-to-back. It can also be downloaded at www.barnabasinchurches.org.uk/9780857463661.)

The costumes

Costumes are not essential, as imagination can fill in the gap. However, most children love dressing up and it adds to the atmosphere of any nativity story. Providing costumes sounds like a lot of work, but it really doesn't have to be, and a wardrobe can be built up and enhanced as each year goes by. You can find a helpful guide to making simple costumes, with as little sewing as possible, on pages 42–49.

I love the idea of children coming pre-dressed in whatever costumes they might have at home, for whatever character they choose, but it does raise one concern. A nativity play can have as many kings, shepherds, innkeepers, sheep, dogs, camels and donkeys as you like, but, if children come dressed as Mary or Joseph, you will have the problem of how to manage multiple main characters. This can lead to disappointment and stress, just at the point when all you want is calm.

To address this:

- Choose children to play Mary and Joseph as early as you can.
- When advertising on posters or through email or website, make sure you emphasise that children are invited to come dressed to join 'this year's Mary and Joseph at our Christingle/nativity service'. By saying 'this year', you will help the children to understand that they could be Mary or Joseph next year and soften any disappointment.

Herod or no Herod?

For the first time in all my years of producing nativity plays, a child came in last Christmas and asked to be Herod. I was not prepared for this, but the child at least pretended to understand when I told him that we wouldn't have time to allow the wise men to travel to Jerusalem. However, just because I don't include Herod, it doesn't mean that you can't.

Real baby or doll?

Dolls are often in abundance where small children are involved, but having the right kind of doll to represent Jesus can be important so that it doesn't distract from the story. It is lovely if a small child offers her favourite doll, but if it is as big as the child or too small to be seen or has long pink hair, it may be distracting. However, you will need to give a careful explanation to a child who has brought in their unsuitable but treasured doll.

In London, as in many other areas, we were part of an international community; therefore, Mary and Joseph could be Indian, Caribbean, Korean, Nigerian, Italian or any other nationality. It might be nice to depict their ethnicity in the doll you use, but it is not essential.

What about including a real baby? For several of our No-Rehearsal Nativities we were thrilled to have newborn or small babies in our congregation at the time. When invited, parents were often equally thrilled for their little ones to play the part of Jesus. However, although parents may feel that it is incredibly special for their baby to play Jesus, some will be nervous that the baby might cry and spoil the event or, even worse, that a young Mary might drop him or her.

Here are a few practical tips to address this issue.

- Ask the baby's parent to play either an angel or villager who brings Mary the baby. The parent is then present while the baby takes centre stage.

- Choose a Mary who is used to handling a baby brother or sister. Have a baby doll ready, just in case the baby needs to go back to his or her real mum.

- Have two Marys and two Josephs, played by one adult and one child for each character. The emphasis will be on the children, but the adults can shadow the children.

Including the Christingle

The Christingle service is separate from the nativity play in many churches, but for many years we have incorporated it into the No-Rehearsal Nativity.

Christingle candles, in their very special holders, were introduced into the Anglican Church in England in the 1960s by the Children's Society, who brought the idea to our shores from Moravia (now part of the Czech Republic).

Churches all over the world give out lighted candles at Christmas to remind us that Jesus is our light and the light of the world. Christingle means 'Christ's light' and is a wonderful visual way of helping children to see that God's light shines over the whole world.

Christingles are easy and great fun to construct, especially if you gather a group of adults and children together to make them. They are also a wonderful way to build the excitement for the nativity.

Symbolism behind the Christingle

Not only does the Christingle look beautiful, but its meaning is beautiful, too.

- The orange represents the world.
- The candle represents Jesus, the light of the world.
- The red ribbon that goes around the orange reminds us that Jesus suffered and died for us, red being the colour of blood.
- The four cocktail sticks represent the four corners of the world, where the four seasons supply our world with its harvest.
- The raisins or sweets represent the gifts of God—his provision, love and kindness, which we are called to enjoy.
- I would like to find a theological reason for the foil, but it is actually there to catch the wax if it drips from the candle. Only aluminium foil should be used, as any other material (such as Christmas wrapping paper) is too risky.

As an alternative to red ribbon, I recommend using 2 cm red electrical tape, available from any hardware store. It is much easier to use than ribbon as it sticks to the orange securely.

When buying cocktail sticks, it is best, for health and safety reasons, to get those that have one blunt tip and one sharp tip.

Sweets look wonderful on the sticks, but remember that providing sweets may be an issue with some parents. If it is likely to cause a problem, you can either use raisins on all your Christingles or have some with raisins available for those who are allergic to sugar.

Making the Christingle

I have found that the easiest way to make Christingles is in conveyor-belt style. For this, you will need at least six volunteers, but the number you are making will determine how many teams you need. Whether it's 20 or 400 Christingles, however, the principle is the same.

- Set up trestle tables and cover them in plastic tablecloths or cut-up bin liners, which you can tape down to keep secure.
- Put the boxes of oranges on the floor at one end of the table.
- Place a tray at the same end, filled with oranges, and trays at the other end to receive the finished Christingles.
- Set out chairs on either side of the table for those who are helping.
- The first person (an adult) uses a sharp knife to cut just enough off the base of the orange in order for it to stand up straight, and passes it down the line.

- The next person makes a small circular hole, using a knife or an apple corer, in the top of the orange to hold the candle. It should not be too wide, as the candle needs to be snug in the hole, but it does need to be at least 1.5 cm deep so that the candle won't fall over.
- The next person takes the orange and carefully places the red tape or ribbon horizontally around the middle. Red electrical tape is perfect as it adheres to the orange.
- The next person takes a candle, stands it in the centre of a pre-cut square piece of aluminium foil, and pushes it gently into the hole in the top of the orange. (Check that the candle is fixed securely in the hole.)
- The next person carefully adds the raisins and/or sweets to the cocktail sticks.
- The last in line pushes the cocktail sticks into the oranges and places the finished Christingle on the tray. (It's important for the sticks to stand as vertical as possible in the top half of the orange. If they are sticking out at right angles from the orange, it is hard to stand the Christingles together on a tray, and can also be dangerous when children are holding the orange.)

Trays are helpful as the finished Christingles look wonderful when placed together, and they make for easy distribution when the time comes.

Candle or battery?

Churches are traditionally happy with the use of candles but the combination of children and candles needs extra special care.

Having bowls of damp towels discreetly and strategically placed around the church means that, if any accident should happen, the people assigned can find the towels quickly. In the many years I have been involved with Christingle services, so far parents and children have all adhered to the instructions and no accident has ever occurred.

However, if you prefer to use battery-powered candles, these can be bought online or wholesale. There are many different kinds and some are incredibly realistic. You might decide to exchange the battery candles for real candles at the end of the service, which children can light under parental supervision at home.

The lighting of candles

When the Christmas story has been told and the children are still in costume, the service can be concluded with the giving and lighting of the Christingles. This is a magical time and can easily be ruined by too much military precision. However, the helpers do need to pay particular attention to ensure that all goes smoothly. Instructions can be given by the church leader or the storyteller and will vary depending on the size of the congregation and geography of the church.

Christingles should be given to all the children at the service, whether or not they have taken part in the nativity, so that they feel included. Ask all the children to come to the place where the church leader and storyteller are standing and form a single circle to receive the Christingles. If yours is a big church with a large number of children and adults, you will need to think how best to do this. It may be that you make a circle around the pews or chairs, filling the whole church.

The circle

Circles are inclusive, but in this case they also promote safety. Ask the parents or carers to bring their children into the circle and ask them to stand behind their own child or children while you give out the Christingles. Only when you have a circle of children with the parents standing behind and on duty to protect their children will you light the candles.

The church leader or storyteller could place Mary, Joseph and baby Jesus at the centre of the circle. If your church has lighting that can be dimmed or turned off when all the candles are lit, the children and congregation can sing 'Away in a manger' by candlelight.

After the song and a final blessing, bring up the lights, blow out the candles and joyfully sing 'We wish you a merry Christmas' to end the service.

Processions

Children love processions but, for safety reasons, I would not recommend them. In the circle, the lit candles are in front of the children, and they are standing still, under adult supervision. In a procession, the children are walking behind others who may have long hair or be wearing scarves, robes and so on. Worries about the lit candles can then distract from the beauty and sensitivity of the moment.

Giving

Christmas is a time for giving, but many of us feel that the secular world encourages children to see it as a season for getting. Of course it is wonderful for children to receive gifts, but it is also wonderful for them to experience the joy that giving brings.

Churches, schools and families can encourage giving in many ways. Giving doesn't need to involve money. Helping around the house, being kind, being a good friend, showing ways of being unselfish, smiling, or being cheerful and responsive are all ways in which we can give. If children have pocket money, they could be encouraged to give away a little of it or be part of the decision-making with parents and carers about how to finance gifts, whether large or small.

The Children's Society does valuable work and is always delighted to receive donations that come from a Christingle service. You can order a Christingle pack from them, containing envelopes for the children to collect money in, either before the event or at the end of the service. The website www.christingle.org also gives information about how to send donations.

Including the blessing of the crib

Like the Christingle, the blessing of the crib is a separate service in many churches but can equally be incorporated into the No-Rehearsal Nativity.

St Francis of Assisi's live nativity scene or 'crèche', first set up around 1223, has been the inspiration for many beautiful and creative nativities all over the world. Francis had been to the Holy Land and seen the birthplace of Jesus. On his return he was passionate about giving people who could not travel to Bethlehem as real an experience as possible of the nativity by bringing the story to life in a dramatic way.

A cave was prepared near the friars' hermitage, complete with manger, ox and ass. Francis was delighted. When evening arrived, villagers came in a candlelit procession, the sound of their singing ringing out through the night air. It is said to have been a night when people rediscovered the joy of a childlike response to God. Their hearts were touched by an understanding of the hardship that Jesus suffered as an infant and the humble status to which God himself chose to be born.

If we can give our children a sense of the enormity of that first Christmas and also live out the desire that Francis had for us to meet God with open and childlike hearts, they will experience a night to remember.

The words 'childlike' and 'childish' can so often be misinterpreted as meaning the same thing. To be childlike is to learn to come to God with openness, trust and wonder, accepting his love without test or demand. Jesus said, 'Truly I tell you, anyone who will not receive the kingdom of God like a little child will never enter it' (Mark 10:15).

Francis wanted us to be childlike, and over the centuries his tradition of depicting the nativity scene has continued. Churches all over the world set up a crib or crèche or stable scene inside their building. Sometimes churches enact nativity scenes with real people depicting the tableau.

There has been a set of nativity figures in all the churches of which I've been a part. Some have been treasured, while others have needed a little tender loving care, and they have usually been carved models of characters from the Christmas story, including animals. In some years, however, we have exchanged the traditional figures for large dressed figures with paper-plate faces or child-sized cone bodies with papier-mâché heads.

Large or small, porcelain or papier mâché, we bring them into the nativity service for several reasons. In the blessing of the crib, children see how important the Christmas story is, because the representation of the story is set up for all to see. Carrying the crib figures or seeing them brought to the crib (if they are precious or fragile) is a way for children to reinforce the connection of the characters in the nativity play to the Bible story. Practically, it is a way to combine the tableau created by the children at the end of the drama with the scene of the crib, set in preparation for its blessing.

Tradition and repetition are important for children, and the crib is something they can always look for in churches, wherever they are at Christmas.

Combining crib and nativity

During the carol 'Oh come all ye faithful', sung when the final tableau of the nativity play is in place, the children can be given the crib figures, which may have been waiting for them on the high altar or table. It may be that the figure of Mary is given to Mary, a shepherd figure to a shepherd, and so on—or you may wish to give the figures to children who you want to make feel special or to those who you are sure won't drop them! The figures will remain with the crib scene for the duration of the Christmas period.

Encouraging everyone to join in

Interacting with the children

Throughout the nativity service, there will be many opportunities to interact and ask the children questions. If you are new to working with children, there are a few things to remember.

- If you ask a question and there is no response, don't panic but come in with a ready answer as if it were perfectly natural.
- It's really important that we never embarrass children by putting them on the spot. Even the most confident child can clam up when finding themselves in front of an audience.
- If a child gives an answer that seems ridiculous, silly or attention-seeking, it is always good to defuse the situation by pretending not to hear and moving on. Always remember that a sarcastic response from you, no matter how well meant, may not be understood by the children and will most likely upset the parents.

Audience participation

I speak of 'audience participation' rather than 'asking the congregation to join in' because we want to feel that the congregation is working with us. For this to happen, it is up to everyone on the team to create an atmosphere in which people feel able to participate—and that means everyone from the welcomers, and those who help the children with their costumes, to the storyteller.

Call-outs

It is only in the last few years that I have introduced participation with 'call-outs' from the congregation—that is, a specific response prompted by the storyteller whenever certain words are spoken. Once I knew the core congregation—the ones who were there every year, who trusted me—I felt I could bring them further into the event so that everyone was together in the telling of the story.

Any call-outs need to be very simple. There is nothing worse in this situation than for the children and congregation to be confused. If they are confused, they will get the response wrong and then it's just embarrassing for everyone. It can be amusing, but you will want everyone to come away focused on what they have experienced, not talking about a mistake so funny that they forgot the Christmas story itself. You will see that the No-Rehearsal Nativity script that follows contains just one call-out.

All of us will know our audiences, and that is something we must keep at the forefront of our minds. If you are just beginning to introduce a nativity play, it may be better to keep simplicity paramount so that you can see how the children and families react, and build on it year by year. If everyone has a wonderful experience, they will come back next year, tell their friends, bring their next child or bring their grandchildren, and your No-Rehearsal Nativity will grow and develop over the years.

On the pages that follow, you will find a suggested script for the No-Rehearsal Nativity. Every storyteller will have their own particular style and, as long as they are joyful, calm, respectful of children and adults alike and have in their hearts the desire to give everyone a close encounter with God, then all will be well.

The No-Rehearsal Nativity script

Welcome

Good evening and a big, big welcome to everyone.

Now can I ask all our wonderful actors to come out and join me?

(Speaking to the children as they arrive) You all look just fantastic and we are so happy that you are here on this very special night.

Well, here we are and it's Christmas Eve—the night before Christmas!

I think there may be a great deal of excitement in your homes at the moment. There may be secret presents being wrapped, special foods waiting to be eaten, and family and friends visiting, but… Why are we here tonight? What are we going to be doing here tonight? What is Christmas all about? Why do we do these special things?

This is a time to take the opportunity to ask questions and interact with children, if appropriate.

The real reason for all the excitement is that tomorrow is the birthday of Jesus and everything we do at Christmas is for him. It is because of him that you will be receiving some presents.

Jesus received some very grown-up presents, given to him by the wise men who visited him as a baby.

I love receiving presents and I love giving them, too. We are given gifts on all sorts of occasions, especially when it's our birthday and at Christmas. Both these times are to do with Jesus, because Christmas Day is his birthday, and, because he was given presents, we remember him by doing the same for each other.

But, you know, a present doesn't have to cost a lot of money, and sometimes the best ones are the ones that cost nothing at all. A big smile for your mum or dad when you wake up is a lovely present. Remembering to say 'thank you' for treats that you are given. Maybe a big hug for Mum when she looks tired, or making a card for Grandma if she is not very well.

Now you being here tonight and us acting out the story of his birth is a big, big present for Jesus, and we all know that he will be thrilled with it.

On that special night, over 2000 years ago, God gave us Jesus—to be born on earth, to grow up and teach us how to love each other, and to help us learn how to be happy and make God's world a wonderful place.

Christingle explanation

If you will be giving out Christingles at the end of the service, this is a good time to introduce them, as it will spoil the moment if you move into an explanation of the Christingle once the play and crib blessing are finished.

The explanation can simply be a straight talk but it also offers a chance to engage everyone and allow the children to talk. It does not have to be done by the storyteller for the play; it is sometimes good to have another voice heard.

Christingle talk

Before our play, I just want to ask you if you know what a Christingle is, because each one of you will be given one to take home. It's called a Christingle because the first part of the word is 'Christ', who is Jesus, and 'ingle' means 'light', so it is a 'Jesus light'.

Why do you think we use an orange? Can you think of something that this round shape reminds you of?

Answers may include a ball or a sweet. Whatever answer is given, always remember to treat it seriously, even if the child is joking. If the right answer is not forthcoming, tell them quickly rather than prolong the situation.

[Answer] The orange is in the shape of the world. But what about this red ribbon/tape that goes all around the world?

Respond to a few answers.

[Answer] Jesus grew up and lived and then died, and the red circle around the world is to show that when he suffered and died, he did so for everyone in the world—for you and me and for everyone who has ever lived.

Now let's think about these four sticks. In our year, what do we have four of? Can anyone think?

[Answer] Seasons! Spring, summer, autumn and winter. And the sweets and raisins, what could they be?

[Answer] In every part of the world, there is a harvest time when all the wonderful foods that God has given us get ripe. God makes them for us to enjoy and so that we stay healthy. Who has a favourite food?

Engage in interaction.

And to crown it all is the candle, to show that Jesus is the one who lights up our lives.

The nativity play

Now it's time for us to tell our story, so let's get ready.

This is the opportunity for the adult actors to gather the children into groups—shepherds, kings and stars, angels, innkeepers, animals, and so on. The angel Gabriel takes Mary and Joseph to their places and leaves them there, making sure they know that he/she will come back to them later.

Now, there were lots of people involved in the story that led up to that night, over 2000 years ago, when Jesus was born, so let's see if we have everyone we need.

Have we got shepherds—kings—and animals (donkeys, sheep and cows)? Do we have our star and angels, Mary, Joseph and innkeepers? Good.

Just before we start, let's see if we can get every single person who is here tonight to join in too.

We all know that lots of truly amazing things happen in our story, so we thought it would be good for everyone to join in whenever we act them out. I mean not only our actors but all the mums, dads, grannies, grandads, aunties, uncles and friends! So when you hear the words '*Truly amazing*', can you all call out, '*Amazing. Wow!*'

And just to make it more fun, when you say 'Amazing. Wow!' can you throw your hands up in the air too? Great! So let's give it a try.

God knows all of us better than we know ourselves, which is *truly amazing*.

Everyone responds, *Amazing. Wow!* **with arms thrown up in the air. If the response was enthusiastic, it doesn't need to be practised again. You can just say, 'What an amazing night we are going to have with support like that. Thank you.' If people need some encouragement, have your adult actors and children primed for a second practice:**

Shall we try that again and see if our young actors can take the lead? I think all the children here look *truly amazing*.

Everyone responds, *Amazing. Wow!* **If you feel that the call-out is just not going to work, either focus on the children's response or leave it out altogether.**

　　Now is the time to send the children off with the adult actors to different places around the church, or just to the side, so that the main stage area can be seen.

Kings, would you like to go to the back of the church, shepherds to the right, angels together over there, innkeepers here, animals there—[and so on]. Now can I ask Mary to come to the centre here, with Joseph sitting a little to her right/left.

Ready?

Now God knew that there was a faithful young girl who lived in Nazareth, whose name was Mary. He knew her very well and they often talked when she prayed. God had chosen Mary to be the mother of his son, Jesus, but he needed to ask her if she would do as he asked.

Let's see if we can find her. There she is! Mary, can you come and sit on the steps here? Lovely. Thank you.

With such an important question to ask, God sent for his top messenger angel, Gabriel. Gabriel, now is the time for you to go and see Mary. Gabriel loved visiting people on earth, especially when he had good news, and this was the best.

Mary was sitting thinking and quietly praying, when suddenly Gabriel appeared.

Gabriel could come in and kneel down by Mary, as long as he can still be seen.

And it was *truly amazing*!

Everyone: *Amazing. Wow!*

Mary was so surprised.

Gabriel: Don't be frightened, Mary. I am one of God's special messengers, and he loves you so much that he has asked me to come and ask you if you will be the mother of his son and name him Jesus.

Mary was a faithful girl and she knew that if God asked her to do anything, she could say 'Yes' because he would take care of her.

But Mary was also thinking about Joseph, the man she was going to marry. Let's find Joseph. Here he is. Joseph, we know that you've had a busy day, so would you like to sit here and have a little sleep? Wonderful.

Gabriel: We don't need to worry about Joseph, because he is *truly amazing*.

Everyone: *Amazing. Wow!*

Gabriel: Mary, you know that God is in Joseph's heart, so I spoke to him in a dream and I am going to go and bring him to you now.

Gabriel goes to find Joseph and brings him over to Mary.

Joseph promised to look after Mary and the baby, but he did have some news that wasn't so good. He told her that they would have to travel to Bethlehem, the town where his family came from. The Roman governor had said that every man must go back to their home town, so that all the people could be counted, and they would have to go at about the time when Mary would be having her baby.

Time flew by and it was soon time for them to leave for Bethlehem. They travelled like many others, with their very special donkey. Where is our donkey? Wonderful, here he/she is.

The donkey, Mary and Joseph started their journey to Bethlehem. There were lots of people travelling to Bethlehem from all over the place and it would take several days to get there. I am sure that Mary found it very difficult and slow going because she was now nearly ready to give birth to Jesus.

To help them along their way, let's all sing the song 'Little donkey'.

During this carol, the travelling actors walk around the church, in order to give the impression that they are arriving in Bethlehem.

Now, because Mary was almost ready to have her baby, they had to travel slowly, so the journey took longer than it did for other people. When they arrived, Joseph sat Mary down and went to ask at some of the hotels if they had any rooms. He needed a safe place for Mary to have the baby, but the people who got there before them had taken all the rooms.

Joseph went to each hotel in turn and said:

Joseph: Please have you got somewhere for my wife to have her baby?

If you have a Joseph and innkeepers who are prepared to speak, they can be encouraged to do so. If they are not easy to hear, either hold a microphone for them or, if this is not possible, simply repeat what they say as if it was supposed to happen that way.

Each time the answer came back:

Innkeeper: Sorry, we really have no room.

Joseph went back to Mary and said:

Joseph: I'm so sorry, Mary, but I can't find anywhere.

Then one of the innkeepers came over to Joseph and said, 'I haven't got a room for you, but I have a stable. It's dry and warm and you are welcome to it.'

Joseph was relieved and said that it was *truly amazing*.

Everyone: *Amazing. Wow!*

Mary and Joseph said 'thank you' and followed the innkeeper to the stable.

Gabriel helps to guide Mary and Joseph and settles them into their tableau positions.

They settled down and got ready for the greatest night of all time. Let's give them a moment and sing a carol that tells the story of that night: 'Silent night'.

During this carol, there is the opportunity to get the shepherds in position. You could have a 'fire' for them to gather round, made very simply with twigs and tissue paper, which one of the adult shepherds can bring on.

Also during the carol, the angel Gabriel can bring in the baby Jesus, if it is a doll, or a real baby can be carried on by its mother, dressed as Mary or an angel. It will be lovely if the young Mary can hold the baby, but, if not, encourage them to be really close.

The angel Gabriel or the leaders of any animals and travellers can gently move them to the manger and encourage them to gather so that they can see and be seen. Make sure space is left for the shepherds and, later, the kings.

Meanwhile, an adult angel gathers the angels together to one side, so that they are ready to run on and surprise the shepherds.

So Jesus was born. While Mary and Joseph looked on, they were surrounded by animals, and all the innkeepers looked in to see baby Jesus in the manger.

Another wonderful thing was happening on the hills outside Bethlehem at the same time.

You see, on that night, there were shepherds looking after their sheep on the hills outside Bethlehem. Their day was over, the sheep were resting and the shepherds had settled around the fire that was burning to keep them warm and keep the wild animals away.

Some of the shepherds were sleepy. Some were cold and some were just fed up, but suddenly, out of nowhere came the sound of singing. The sky was filled with angels.

At this point, the pianist or organist should play the carol 'Angels from the realms of glory' at full volume. During the carol, the angels run and dance together up to the front of the church and surround the shepherds in a semicircle, leaving the front open.

The shepherds were terrified, as none of them had ever seen an angel, and none of them could imagine why the angels would come to them. It was *truly amazing*.

Everyone: *Amazing. Wow!*

Then the angels actually spoke to them and said, 'You have no need to be afraid. You are very special to God. He has sent us to tell you that he wants you to be the first to meet the baby, his son, who has been born into our world to save us and to show us how to live and how to love. So are you ready for the message? Hurry down to Bethlehem. The baby has been born in a stable, not a grand house, and will be lying in a manger. So come on! Hurry up! Go and see him and worship him.'

The shepherds were still stunned, but they got up and hurried to Bethlehem, not knowing whether to be more amazed that the Saviour of the world was a tiny baby born in a stable in Bethlehem or that they had been chosen to see him first.

All sing the carol 'The first nowell'. The shepherds quickly make their way to the manger, perhaps walking around the church, led by their adult shepherd, and arriving by the end of the carol to see the baby Jesus.

Also during the carol the kings can be getting ready at the back of the church. The procession of the kings can often be long, as lots of children like dressing as kings. (We don't know how many magi there were, so the number doesn't matter.) If you have a child dressed as the star, make sure they are at the back of the church, ready to lead the kings in.

Not only had the poor shepherds been chosen, but wise men from far away, whom we sometimes call 'kings', had also been called to come and see Jesus. They were men who studied the stars and, for them, God did something *truly amazing*.

Everyone: *Amazing. Wow!*

God set a huge star in the sky.

If there is a child who is either dressed as a star or carrying a star, point them out at the back of the church.

Can we all see the star? I think that, just as on that special night it came to rest over the place where Jesus was born, it will come and do that for us in a minute.

The beautiful star was first seen by the wise men, a long time before Jesus was born, and they came hundreds of miles, following it all the way to Bethlehem. Now that is *truly amazing*.

Everyone: *Amazing. Wow!*

I think that those travelling wise men are coming closer, so let's sing their song and wait for them to arrive.

Sing the carol 'We three kings'. During the first verse, see if your star can travel alone to Mary and Joseph and stand either behind, between or beside them.

Dramatically it works well if the kings walk slowly up the aisle, one at a time, during the verses that refer to them. If you have an adult to accompany each one, to set the pace, so much the better. It's hard to get children to walk slowly but it's wonderful if they can. If you have lots of kings, divide them into three groups, setting each group off separately, in time with the different verses.

If you can ask your pianist/organist to pause between the verses so that the storyteller can welcome each king, this really adds to the occasion.

(Before verse 1) See the star coming!

(Before verse 2) Now let's welcome our king who brings gold to show that Jesus is king of our lives and our hearts.

(Before verse 3) Coming next is our king bringing frankincense—beautiful sweet-smelling incense, used in temples and now in churches. It shows that Jesus is our priest as well as our king.

(Before verse 4) Last comes our king bringing myrrh, which was used as an ointment when people died. As we know now, Jesus was going to suffer for us.

(Before verse 5) Let's wonder at the kings who came from far and wide to worship Jesus.

Well, there we are. Let's look at this glorious picture we have in front of us. We have Mary—Joseph—travellers—innkeepers—angels—animals—shepherds—kings—and us. All of us have imagined that we were at the manger in Bethlehem 2000 years ago, to thank God for the birth of Jesus, who is the reason for everything. It's *truly amazing*.

Everyone: *Amazing. Wow!*

And let's give our wonderful actors a huge round of applause to thank them for bringing Christmas to us in such a special way. I'm sure you'll agree, so please join me in loud appreciation when I say that the children have been *truly amazing*.

Everyone: *Amazing. Wow!*

If you are to finish with a crib blessing, carry on with the script. If not, move on to the lighting of the Christingles.

Let's all celebrate by singing 'O come, all ye faithful'. While we sing this carol, the children are going to come up to the altar/table to collect the crib figures. As we bring them down, please come and join us and gather around the crib.

Sing 'O come, all ye faithful'. When all the children are gathered around the crib and have placed the characters in their places, try to manoeuvre Mary and Joseph near to the crib to reinforce the picture. In my experience, it is at this point that the vicar or minister takes over.

Prayer and blessing of the crib

CRIB PRAYER

Let us pray that God our Father will bless this crib and that all who worship his Son, born of the Virgin Mary, may come to share his life in glory.

God our Father, on this night/day your Son Jesus Christ was born of the virgin Mary for us and for our salvation.

Bless this crib, which we have prepared to celebrate that holy birth; may all who see it be strengthened in faith and receive that fullness of life he came to bring, who lives and reigns for ever and ever. Amen

BLESSING

Loving Father, help us remember the birth of Jesus,
that we may share in the song of the angels,
the gladness of the shepherds,
and worship of the wise men.

Close the door of hate and open the door of love all over the world.

May the Christmas morning make us happy to be thy children,
and Christmas evening bring us to our beds with grateful thoughts,
forgiving and forgiven, for Jesus' sake. Amen

A CHRISTMAS PRAYER BY ROBERT LOUIS STEVENSON

The lighting of the Christingles

The storyteller or church leader now asks the children to go with them to an open space in the church. If the geography of the church will not allow this, ask them to make a circle round the church, with their accompanying adults standing behind them.

Once the children are in position, the Christingles can be given out by the team. (It is handy if the Christingles are on trays.) When everyone has one, a team with tapers can light the candles.

When all the Christingles are lit, dim the lights or turn some off to encourage a moment of silence. Candles fascinate most children, and you might be able to manage 20 seconds of pure silence during which the children can be encouraged to say their own prayers. Of course, with so many young children and babies, silence is a challenge, but it is magical when it happens.

Christingle hymns and songs can be incorporated into this part of the service. Further details can be found on the Children's Society website: www.childrenssociety.org.uk.

Sing the carol 'Away in a manger'. As the last line of the carol is sung, bring up the lights, blow out the candles, wish everyone a happy Christmas and burst into 'We wish you a merry Christmas'. Then thank the children, gather them up and, with as many parents as possible, take them off to get changed.

The farewell to all who have attended is very important. Children need to know that they have done well, and should all be thanked for what they have given and receive a personal 'Happy Christmas'. If any of the children are visitors, let them know that everyone is looking forward to their next visit.

The (Almost) No-Sew Nativity

I wish I could truly call this section the 'No-Sew Nativity', but it is more accurate to add the word 'almost'!

You may be fortunate enough to have a wonderful seamstress or tailor in your church who will enjoy making your No-Rehearsal Nativity costumes. If you haven't, and the idea of providing costumes causes you concern, let me say that I have no skill in sewing and yet I have managed to create costumes that have the Wow factor and that children love to wear. It may be my theatrical background, but I think that if you have imagination and an eye for colour, then you too can create costumes.

Although children love to dress up, it is important to do all we can to help them to feel special and not comical. The play is not a fashion parade, but we want our children to look forward to dressing up and not be in any way embarrassed. We sometimes forget that when we laugh because a child looks adorable, the child may misunderstand and think that they look stupid; this is definitely something to avoid.

Adapt and wear

It is amazing what you can find in your own wardrobe that could be transformed into a nativity costume. Try asking your congregation to search through their wardrobes; what comes forth might well be a revelation.

Although it is always gratifying when you are given material or clothes to adapt, I always try to keep to plain or striped fabrics, avoiding things like rose-patterned scarves, in order for the children to feel and look appropriate.

In one of our churches we discovered a host of stored surplices and cottas from days gone by. With the help of stain remover and elastic sewn into the necklines, we made the most amazing set of angel costumes. The short cottas were perfect for our two-year-old angels and the surplices made floor-length costumes for the ten- and eleven-year-olds.

Scarves and pashminas are also useful for making headpieces, belts and tabards. Also take a look when you are passing remnant boxes in fabric shops, as you can often pick up some wonderful bargains.

Don't dismiss a piece of adaptable clothing just because it has sleeves that are too long or a collar and buttons that are inappropriate. Imagine what it could look like with just a few adjustments.

- Try stripping down a man's shirt. See in your mind's eye the collar and buttons removed, the sleeves shortened and the front stitched up to make a long-sleeved tunic.
- What about giving an evening top the same treatment to create a costume for a king, or open up a dress to make a coat?

Some of the most exciting costumes we have made were from adult clothes that had been adapted and cut down to size.

Costume creation time

The section that follows gives some simple and effective techniques for creating basic costumes, which can then be adorned as you like. Measurements will depend, of course, on the sizes of the children and the materials you have at your disposal, but the same basic shapes can be reworked for adults as well as children.

Note

The main reason to have a costumed adult with each of the groups is to give the children confidence, but I also think that, because they have been good enough to enter into the spirit of the occasion, it is important for them to look appropriate and not feel the least bit embarrassed.

With regard to sizing, it is better for costumes to be too big than too small. I strongly advise that all the costumes are made big enough to be worn over the top of the children's own clothes. You may have to turn up their sleeves or turn their collars in, but always insist that they keep their own clothes on, to keep both them and yourselves safe in terms of child protection and general feelings of well-being.

Basic tunic 1

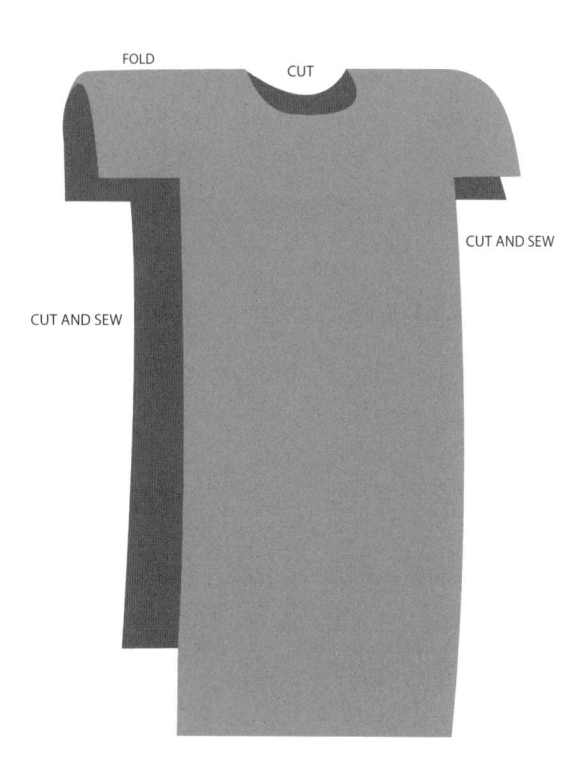

Take your material and fold it in half widthways, with the open end of the cloth at the bottom.

Cut away two rectangular pieces from the sides of the tunic, front and back, so that the basic shape looks as shown above.

It is important not to cut too much away, as you will need to accommodate all sizes of children and everyone needs enough material in the costume to allow them to walk freely.

With the material inside out, sew the sides together and continue to sew along the underarm of the sleeve, which is at a right angle to the sides.

For the neck opening, turn the material inside out and fold it in half, cutting a shallow half circle to make room for the head. It is better to make the opening fairly small, as if it is too big the costume can slip off the shoulders. If you think the opening will be too small to go over the head, cut a vertical slit into the centre of the neck at the back and sew a ribbon to each side that can be tied to hold the neck piece together.

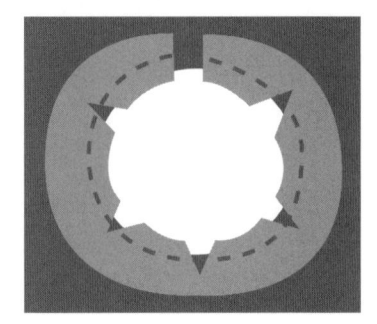

NECK OPENING

If you want to tidy up the neck line, you can fold a piece of ribbon over it, either sewing it on or using iron-on wonderweb to secure it. The ribbon may need a little pleating to make it sit well. Alternatively, you could cut out triangles as shown in the diagram and either tack or wonderweb them in place.

Another option is to add a facing made from material scraps. Cut out a ring shape, a little bigger than the neck opening. Turn the robe inside out, sew the two pieces together, then iron and turn the right way once again.

Basic tunic 2

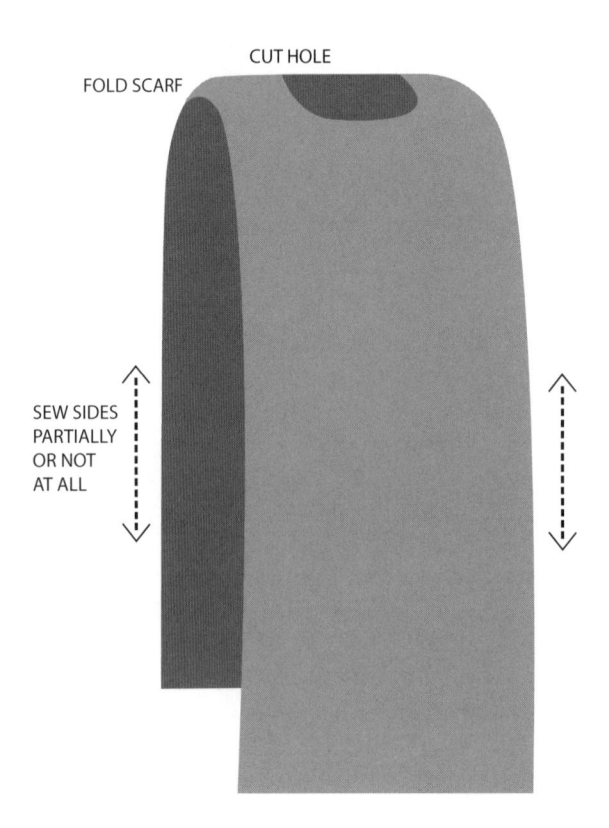

FOLD SCARF
CUT HOLE
SEW SIDES PARTIALLY OR NOT AT ALL

I love this pattern because all that is needed is a long rectangular piece of material. The pashmina-type scarves often sold cheaply in markets make excellent tunics as they need no hemming. I usually cut the fringes off as I have found that they get caught on things and children can find them a distraction.

This tunic can be mixed and matched with other costumes to make it more exciting. It's all about colour and decoration.

Overtunic/Cloak 1

FOLD

CUT OUT CENTRE SECTION

This is my favourite costume piece, especially if it uses a material that doesn't fray, for then it is truly a no-sew garment.

Simply fold over a piece of material, making it the length you wish. Then cut out a central panel, the width of the child's or adult's neck.

Tie a scarf or cord around the waist—either around the whole costume to secure the front flaps, or around the back only, leaving the flaps to flow free.

This item can be worn on top of any of the tunics, and, with the right colours and fabric, can be dressed up or down depending on whether it is for a king or a shepherd.

Overtunic/Cloak 2

For a cloak that flows free at the back, simply add a belt to the Basic Tunic 2. Tie the belt round the child's waist at the back, under the tunic, and secure it over the tunic at the front.

Kaftan

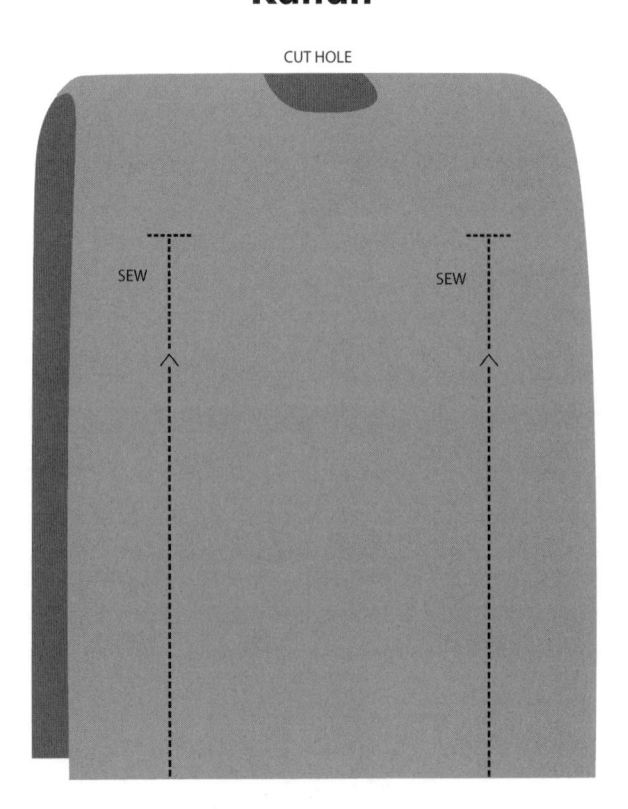

CUT HOLE

SEW   SEW

For a costume that is more loose-fitting than a basic tunic, use a wider piece of material. Fold it in half and cut out an opening at the top, for the neck.

Sew a seam on each side, about three-quarters of the way up the length of the fabric, starting at the bottom. Remember to leave enough space at the top for the child or adult to move freely.

Once again, this garment can be used for any character, dressed up or down, adorned or left plain.

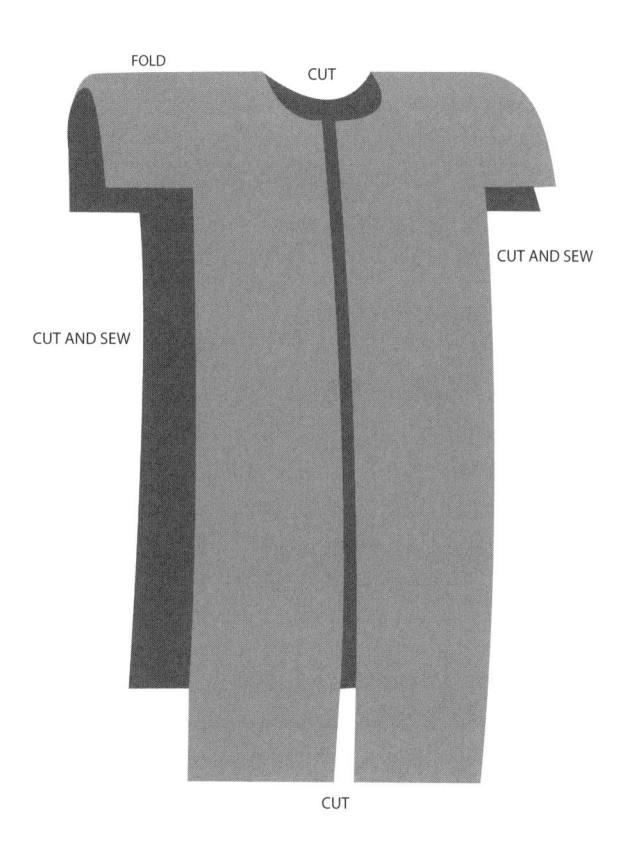

Coat

For a coat, use a basic tunic or kaftan pattern and make a cut all the way up the front, from the bottom to the neck opening.

Angel wings

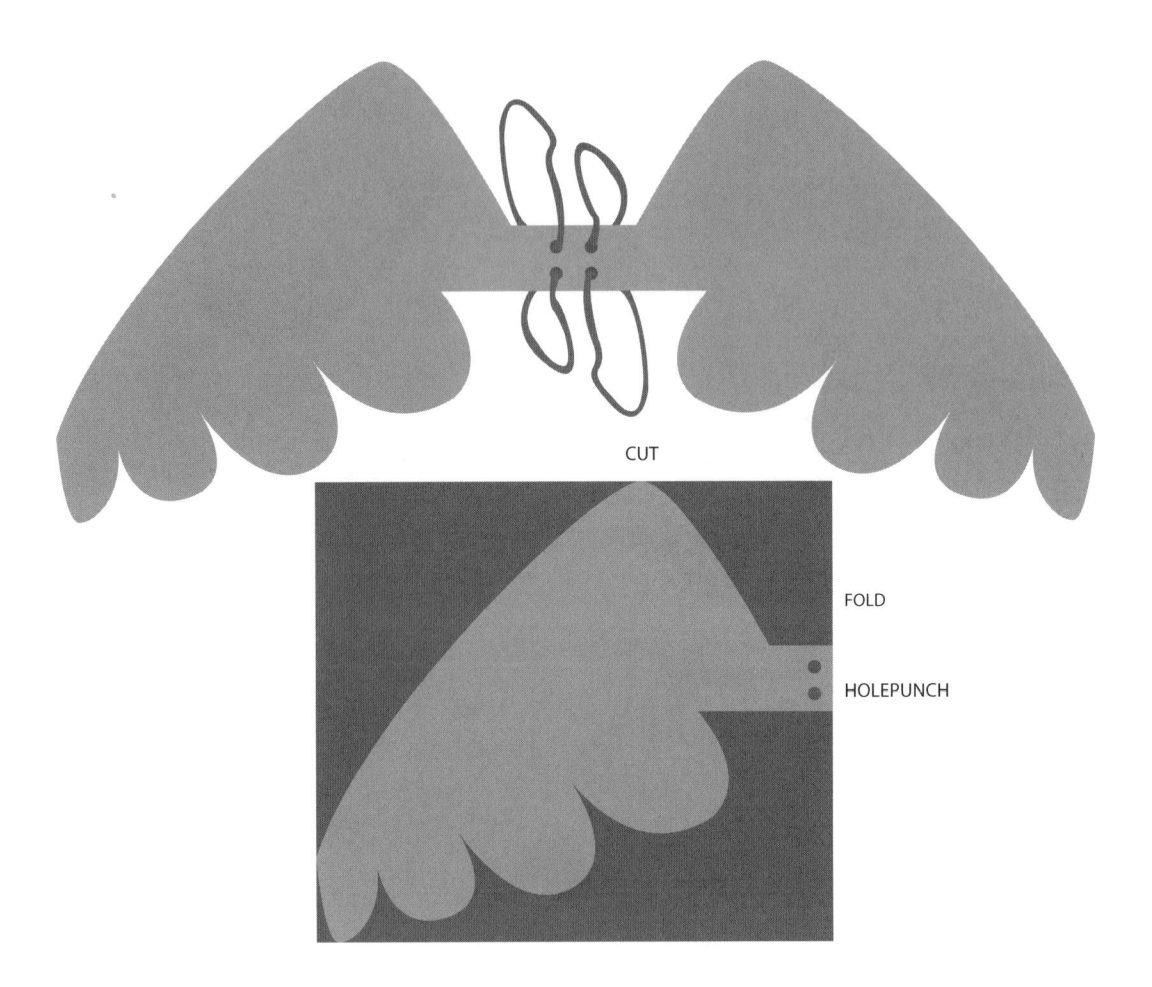

CUT

FOLD

HOLEPUNCH

You may not need to provide your heavenly host with wings if your angel costumes have wide sleeves. When outstretched, such sleeves can work beautifully. However, if you do want wings, the easiest solution I have found is to use thick gold or silver card, which can be covered in feathers if you have the time. Avoid glitter, as, no matter how careful your angels are, they will scatter it wherever they go. I have often still been sweeping glitter up from carpets in March.

Note

Although I don't tend to dress angels in wings, I would never turn away a pair of wings that come attached to a child who has brought her costume from home.

Headdresses

How do you keep headdresses on? Here are two simple solutions. Either stitch elastic into a circle or make headbands using the following method, which I remember from the TV programme *Blue Peter*.

Make a collection of washed tights and cut off the tops and feet, leaving the legs only. Then knot three of the legs together at the top, or sew the tops together, and plait them, tying or sewing up the opposite end. These bands work really well as they have some give in them, look good and, with the variety of colours available, can make a more interesting feature than the serviceable elastic. Try a blue-and-white mix for Mary, browns for the shepherds and black for the kings.

Even if you choose this method, always have elastic to hand as you help to costume the children. I recommend always having plenty of these bands, as all the children will need to feel secure.

The shepherds' fire

A 'fire' is a lovely thing to have at hand as it gives the shepherds a focal point to sit around. It can be simple or elaborate; however, I would suggest that it is made from something that can be easily carried, and not so large that it obscures the children or becomes a scene-stealer.

A round wooden tray with sticks and red tissue paper glued to it looks effective, and you can add battery torches and glow sticks. It is not a good idea to use a tray that you treasure.

Note

The adult shepherd may need a gentle reminder to take responsibility for the fire, as it is one of very few props being used.

Appendices

No-Rehearsal Nativity service sheet

Welcome

Carol: *O come, all ye faithful*

O come, all ye faithful,
Joyful and triumphant,
O come ye, O come ye to Bethlehem.
Come and behold him,
Born the king of angels:

O come, let us adore him,
O come, let us adore him,
O come, let us adore him,
Christ the Lord.

The story of Christingles

The story of Christmas presented by us all

God of God,
Light of light,
Lo, he abhors not the virgin's womb.
Very God,
Begotten, not created.

Chorus

Sing, choirs of angels,
Sing in exultation;
Sing, all ye citizens of heaven above!
Glory to God
In the highest.

Chorus

Procession to the crib

Prayer

Carol: *Away in a manger*

Away in a manger,
No crib for a bed,
The little Lord Jesus
Laid down his sweet head.
The stars in the bright sky
Looked down where he lay,
The little Lord Jesus
Asleep on the hay.

The cattle are lowing,
The baby awakes,
But little Lord Jesus
No crying he makes.
I love thee, Lord Jesus,
Look down from the sky
And stay by my side
Until morning is nigh.

Be near me, Lord Jesus,
I ask thee to stay
Close by me for ever,
And love me, I pray.
Bless all the dear children
In thy tender care
And fit us for heaven
To live with thee there.

Silence

Blessing

Song: *We wish you a merry Christmas*

We wish you a merry Christmas,
We wish you a merry Christmas,
We wish you a merry Christmas
And a happy New Year.

Reproduced with permission from *The No-Rehearsal Nativity* by Janine Gillion (Barnabas for Children, 2015) www.barnabasinchurches.org.uk

Carol: Little donkey

Little donkey, little donkey,
On the dusty road,
Got to keep on plodding onwards
With your precious load.

Been a long time, little donkey,
Through the winter's night.
Don't give up now, little donkey,
Bethlehem's in sight.

Ring out those bells tonight,
Bethlehem, Bethlehem,
Follow that star tonight,
Bethlehem, Bethlehem.

Little donkey, little donkey,
Had a heavy day.
Little donkey, carry Mary
Safely on her way.

Carol: Silent night

Silent night, holy night,
All is calm, all is bright
Round yon virgin mother and child,
Holy infant so tender and mild.
Sleep in heavenly peace,
Sleep in heavenly peace.

Silent night, holy night,
Shepherds quake at the sight.
Glories stream from heaven afar,

Heavenly hosts sing 'Alleluia!'
Christ, the Saviour, is born,
Christ, the Saviour, is born.

Silent night, holy night,
Son of God, love's pure light
Radiant beams from thy holy face
With the dawn of redeeming grace,
Jesus, Lord, at thy birth,
Jesus, Lord, at thy birth.

Carol: Angels from the realms of glory

Angels from the realms of glory,
Wing your flight o'er all the earth;
Ye who sang creation's story
Now proclaim Messiah's birth.

Chorus: Come and worship
Christ, the newborn King;
Come and worship,
Worship Christ, the newborn King!

Shepherds, in the fields abiding,
Watching o'er your flocks by night,
God with man is now residing,
Yonder shines the infant light.

Chorus

Sages, leave your contemplations,
Brighter visions beam afar;
Seek the great desire of nations,
Ye have seen his natal star.

Chorus

Saints before the altar bending,
Watching long in hope and fear,
Suddenly the Lord, descending,
In his temple shall appear.

Chorus

Carol: The first nowell

The first nowell the angel did say
Was to certain poor shepherds in fields as they lay;
In fields where they lay keeping their sheep
On a cold winter's night that was so deep.

Chorus: Nowell, Nowell,
Nowell, Nowell,
born is the King of Israel.

They looked up and saw a star
Shining in the east beyond them far,
And to the earth it gave great light,
And so it continued both day and night.

Chorus

And by the light of that same star
Three wise men came from country far;
To seek for a king was their intent,
And to follow the star wherever it went.

Chorus

This star drew nigh to the north-west,
O'er Bethlehem it took its rest,
And there it did both stop and stay
right over the place where Jesus lay.

Chorus

Then entered in those wise men three
Full reverently upon their knee,
And offered there in his presence
Their gold, and myrrh, and frankincense.

Chorus

Then let us all with one accord
Sing praises to our heavenly Lord;
Who hath made heaven and earth
of nought,
and with his blood mankind hath bought.

Chorus

Carol: We three kings of Orient are

We three kings of Orient are;
Bearing gifts, we traverse afar;
Field and fountain, moor and mountain,
Following yonder star.

Chorus: O star of wonder, star of light,
Star with royal beauty bright,
Westward leading, still proceeding,
Guide us to thy perfect light.

Pause to introduce Melchior

Born a king on Bethlehem's plain,
Gold I bring to crown him again:
King for ever, ceasing never,
Over us all to reign.

Chorus

Pause to introduce Caspar

Frankincense to offer have I;
Incense owns a deity nigh;
Prayer and praising, voices raising,
Worshipping God on high.

Chorus

Pause to introduce Balthazar

Myrrh is mine, its bitter perfume
Breathes a life of gathering gloom;
Sorrowing, sighing, bleeding, dying,
Sealed in the stone-cold tomb.

Chorus

Glorious now behold him arise,
King and God and sacrifice.
'Alleluia, alleluia'
Sounds through the earth and skies.

Chorus

Carol: O come, all ye faithful

O come, all ye faithful,
Joyful and triumphant,
O come ye, O come ye to Bethlehem.
Come and behold him,
born the king of angels.

Chorus: O come, let us adore him,
O come, let us adore him,
O come, let us adore him,
Christ the Lord.

Costume diagrams

These diagrams can also be downloaded at www.barnabasinchurches.org.uk/9780857463661.

Basic tunic 1

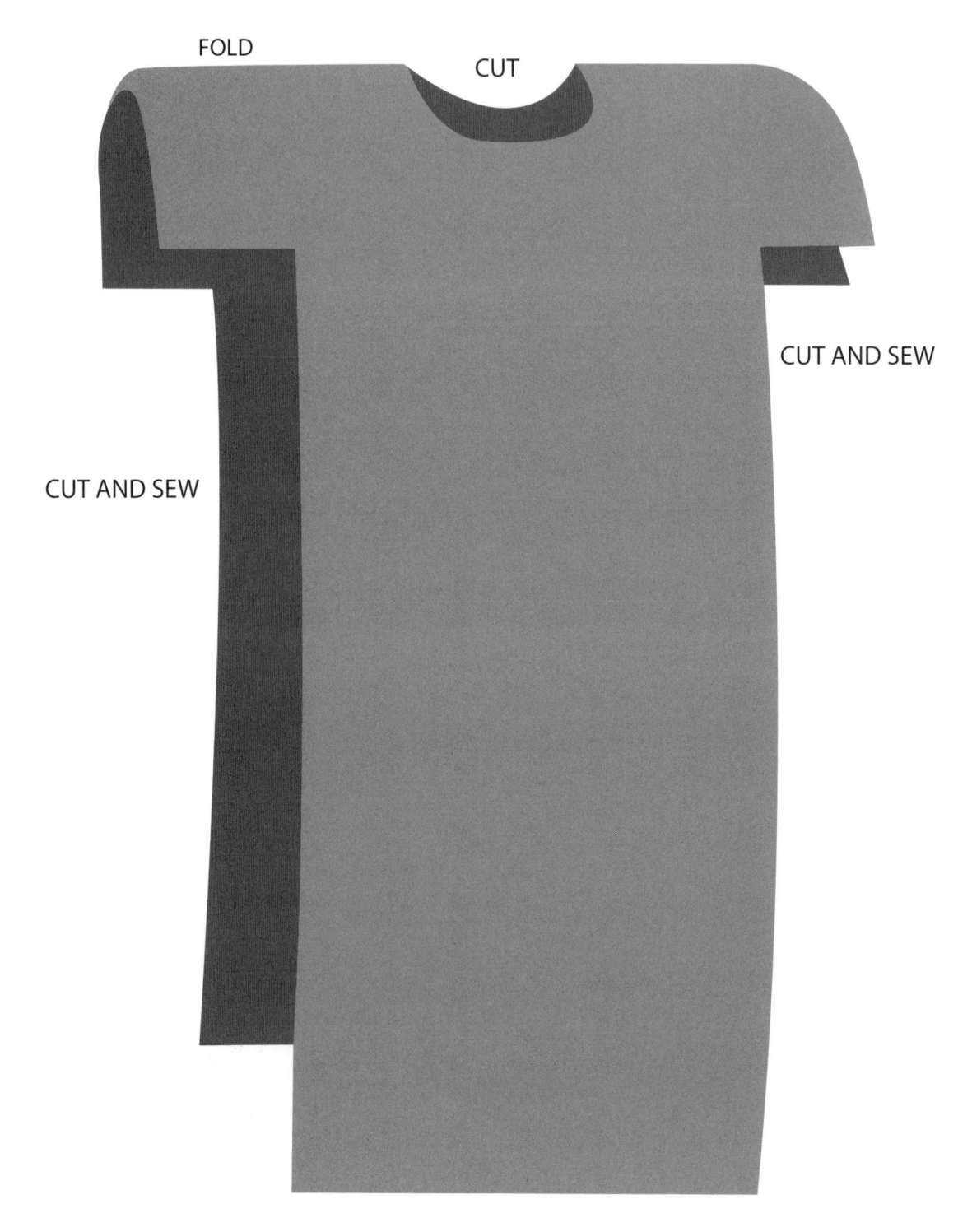

FOLD

CUT

CUT AND SEW

CUT AND SEW

54 Reproduced with permission from *The No-Rehearsal Nativity* by Janine Gillion
(Barnabas for Children, 2015) www.barnabasinchurches.org.uk

Basic tunic 2

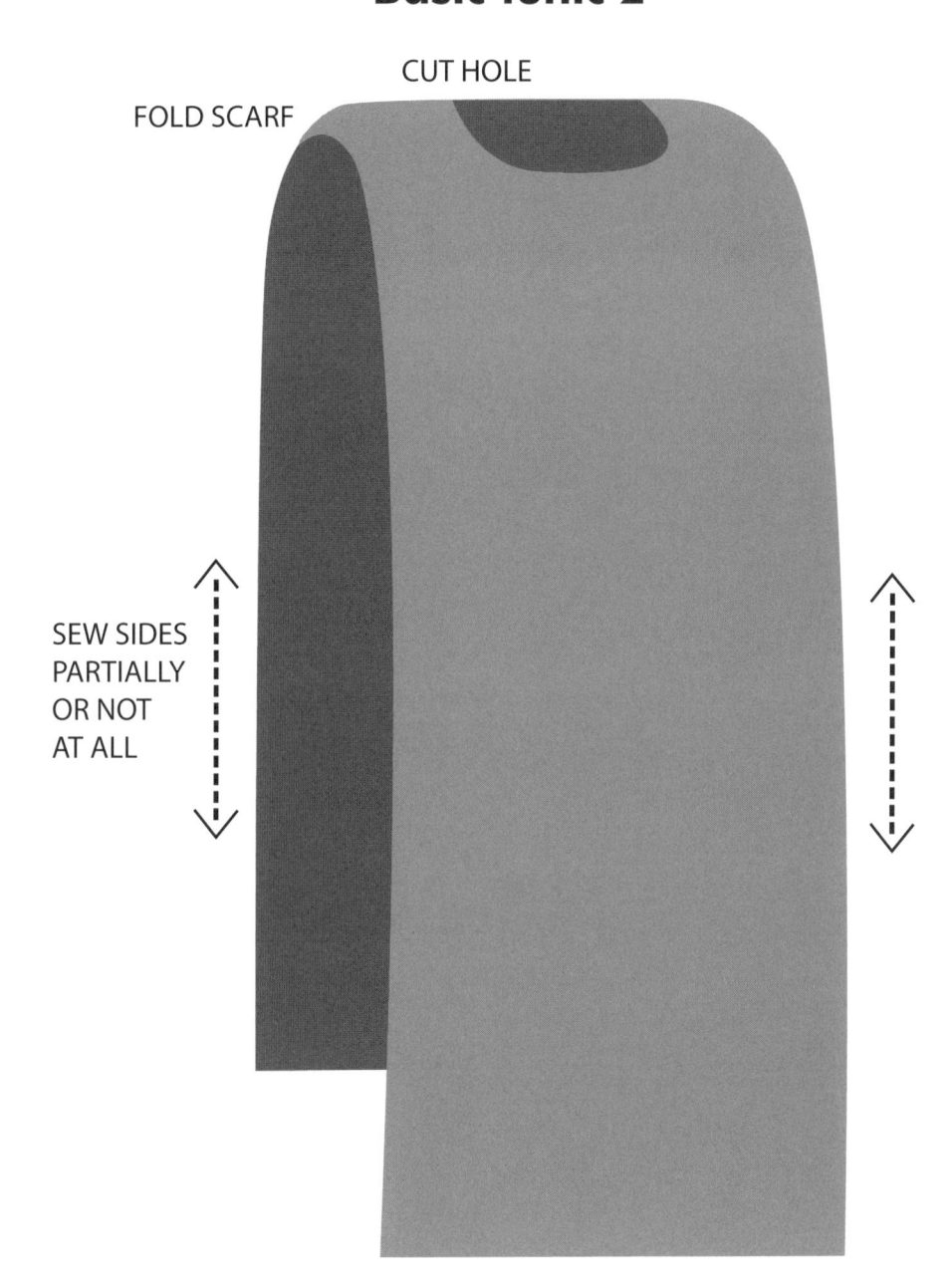

FOLD SCARF CUT HOLE

SEW SIDES PARTIALLY OR NOT AT ALL

Neck opening

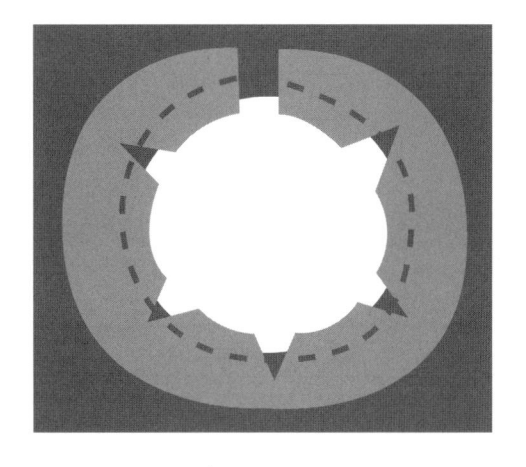

Reproduced with permission from *The No-Rehearsal Nativity* by Janine Gillion (Barnabas for Children, 2015) www.barnabasinchurches.org.uk

55

Overtunic / Cloak 1

FOLD

CUT OUT CENTRE SECTION

Overtunic / Cloak 2

Reproduced with permission from *The No-Rehearsal Nativity* by Janine Gillion (Barnabas for Children, 2015) www.barnabasinchurches.org.uk

Kaftan

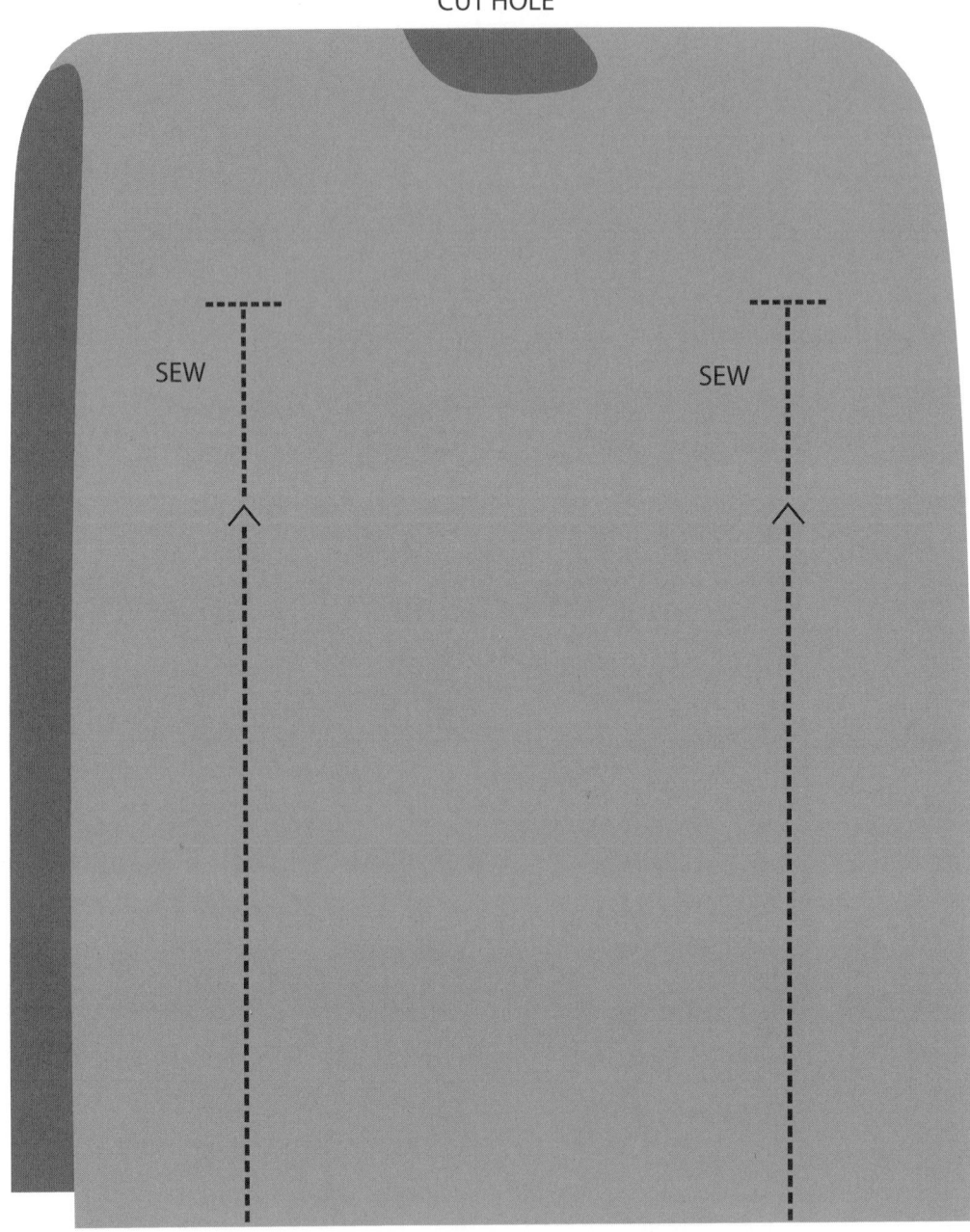

CUT HOLE

SEW　　　　　　　　　SEW

Coat

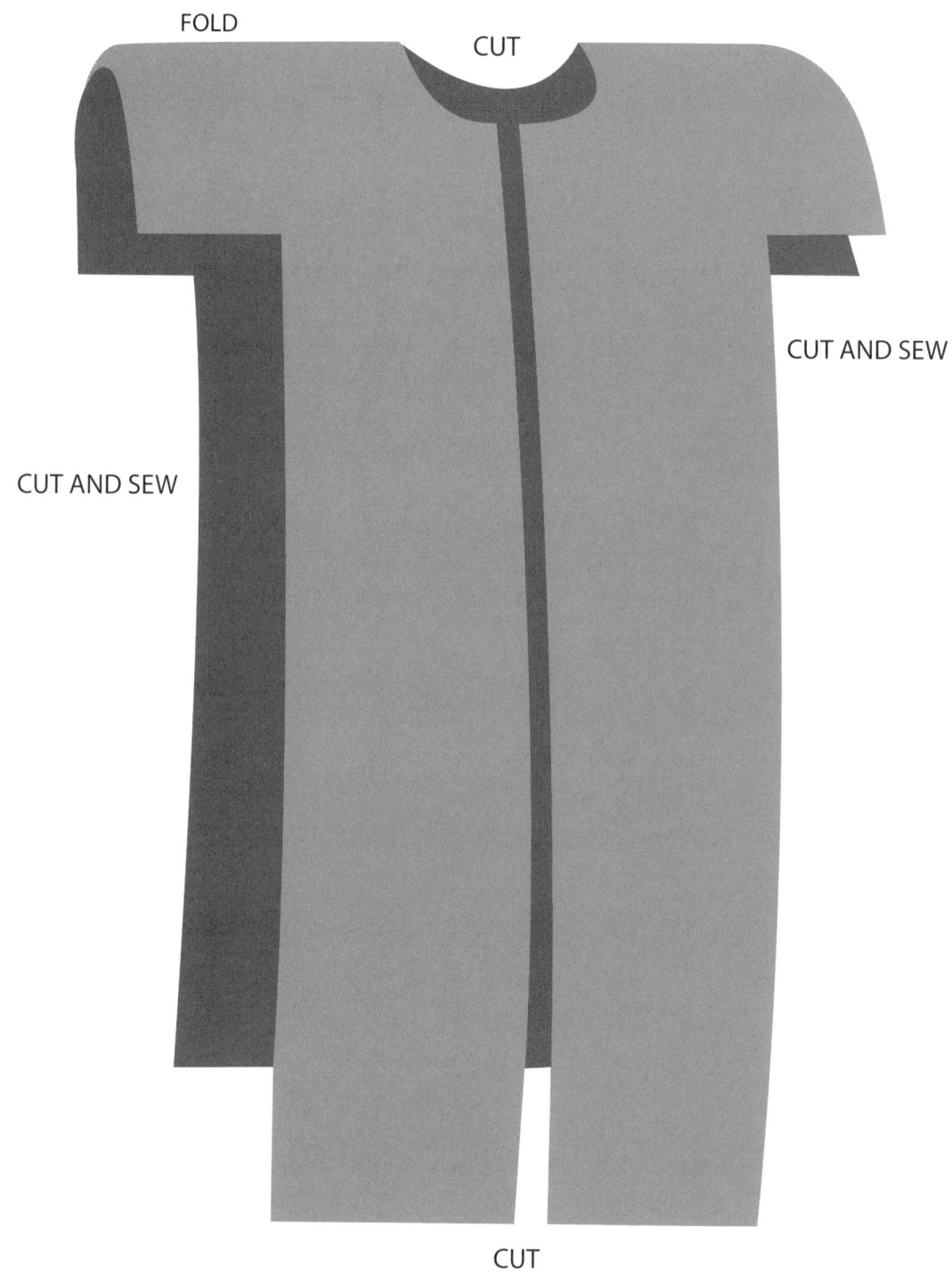

FOLD

CUT

CUT AND SEW

CUT AND SEW

CUT

Reproduced with permission from *The No-Rehearsal Nativity* by Janine Gillion 59
(Barnabas for Children, 2015) www.barnabasinchurches.org.uk

Angel wings

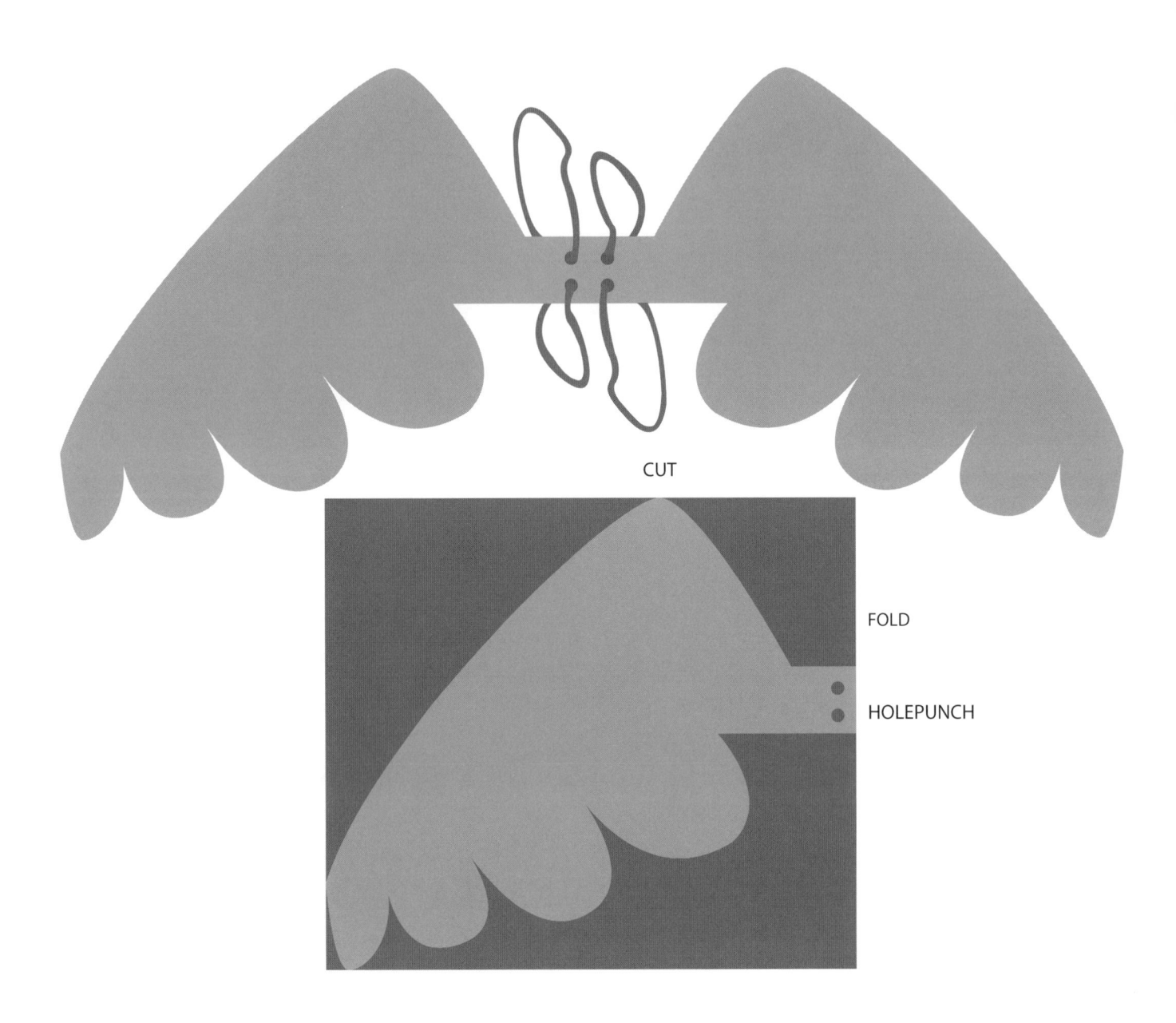

CUT

FOLD

HOLEPUNCH

60 Reproduced with permission from *The No-Rehearsal Nativity* by Janine Gillion
(Barnabas for Children, 2015) www.barnabasinchurches.org.uk

More nativity resources from Barnabas for Children

www.barnabasinchurches.org.uk

The Gingerbread Nativity
ISBN 978 0 85746 161 2
£6.99
96 pages

Messy Nativity
ISBN 978 0 85746 055 4
£4.99
64 pages

101 Christmas Activities
ISBN 978 1 84101 721 1
£5.99
48 pages

Ten Minute Christmas Activity Book
ISBN 978 0 85746 137 7
£3.99
48 pages

Counting Down to Christmas
ISBN 978 1 84101 723 5
£4.99
32 pages

Enjoyed this book?

Write a review—we'd love to hear what you think. Email: reviews@brf.org.uk

Keep up to date—receive details of our new books as they happen.
Sign up for email news and select your interest groups at:
www.brfonline.org.uk/findoutmore/

Follow us on Twitter @brfonline

By post—to receive new title information by post (UK only), complete the form below and post to: BRF Mailing Lists, 15 The Chambers, Vineyard, Abingdon, Oxfordshire, OX14 3FE

Your Details
Name _____
Address _____
_____
Town/City _____ Post Code _____
Email _____

Your Interest Groups (*Please tick as appropriate)
❏ Advent/Lent ❏ Messy Church
❏ Bible Reading & Study ❏ Pastoral
❏ Children's Books ❏ Prayer & Spirituality
❏ Discipleship ❏ Resources for Children's Church
❏ Leadership ❏ Resources for Schools

Support your local bookshop
Ask about their new title information schemes.